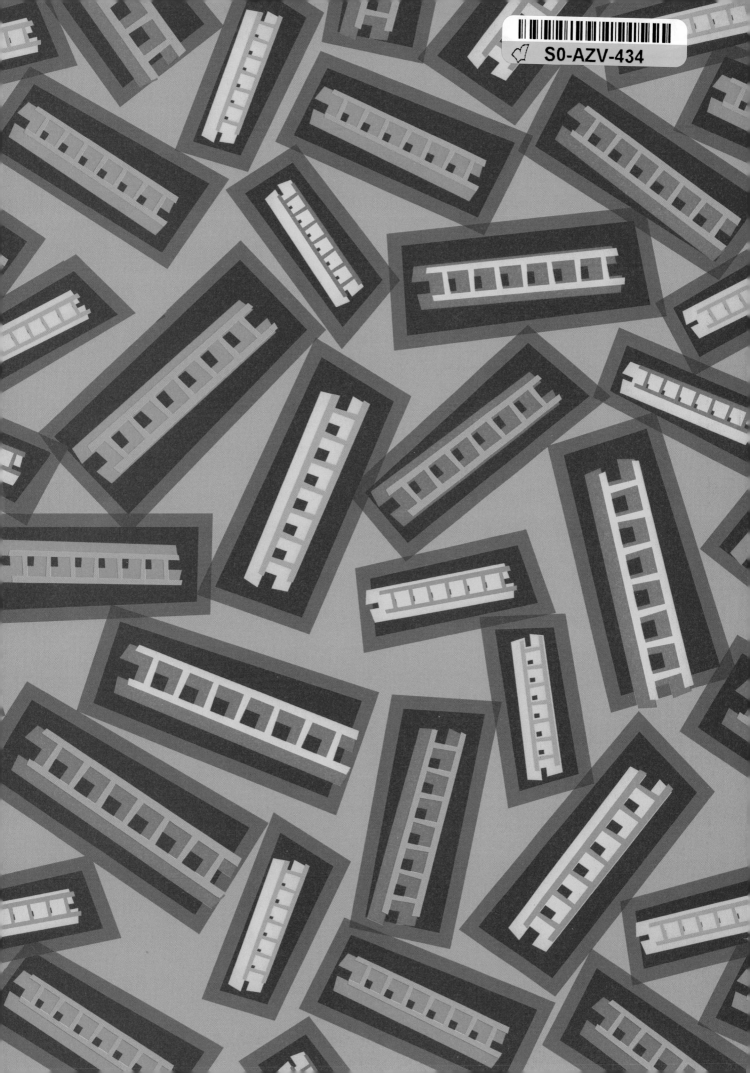

This
Fireman Sam Annual
belongs to

....

....

Nee Nah!

Annual 2008

Contents

Fireman Sam and his family	8
The emergency crew	10
Pontypandy people	12
The Beast of Pontypandy	14
Walkie-talkies	22
King of the jungle	24
Hot stuff!	32
Fit for nothing	34
Trouble and squeak	38
Norman's colouring fun	46
Fiery finale	48
Sam's picture puzzle	56
Mummy's little darling	58
The big freeze	60
Sam's quiz	68

EGMONT
We bring stories to life

First published in Great Britain 2007 by Egmont UK Ltd
239 Kensington High Street, London W8 6SA

Copyright © 2007 S4C International and Prism Art and Design Limited,
a Hit Entertainment company.

Stories adapted from original scripts by Les Brooksbank, Robin Lyons and Annie Smith

ISBN 978 1 4052 3170 1
3 5 7 9 10 8 6 4 2
Printed in Italy

S4/C

Fireman Sam and his family

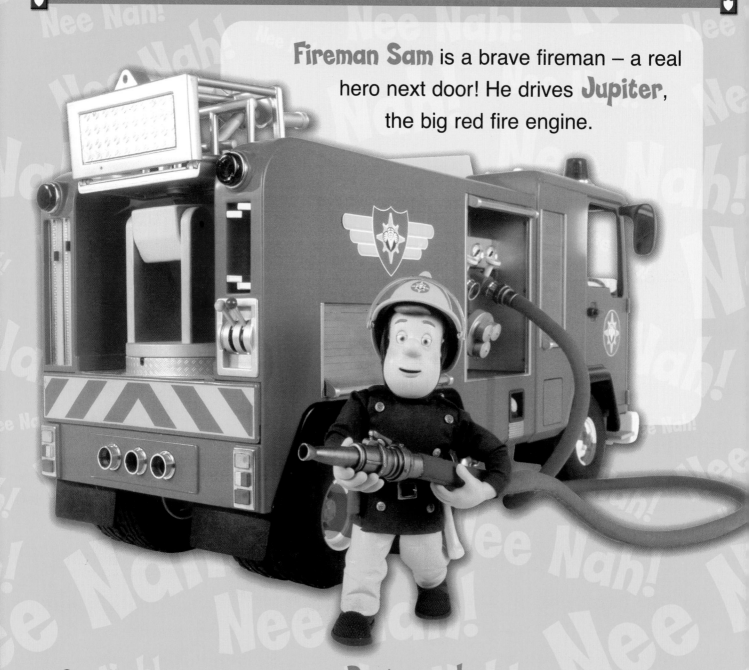

Fireman Sam is a brave fireman – a real hero next door! He drives **Jupiter**, the big red fire engine.

Sam lives in a little town called **Pontypandy**. It's a very friendly place, where everyone knows everyone else.

When he's not on duty at the fire station, Sam spends a lot of time in his shed. He invents all kinds of things in there! You can read about one of them later on.

Sam spends a lot of time with his niece, Sarah, and his nephew James. They're twins, and they both want to be firefighters when they grow up, just like Uncle Sam!

Sarah is always very neat and tidy. She's very sensible and doesn't often get up to mischief.

James will try anything! He loves having fun and adventures. When he won't do as she says, Sarah says he's stubborn!

Dusty the dog doesn't belong to anyone. But everyone in Pontypandy helps look after him.

The emergency crew

The officer in charge of the Pontypandy Fire Station is **Station Officer Steele**. He likes his team to follow his rules. Read about when he took part in the talent show on page 48.

Venus is the Pontypandy rescue tender. Her driver is **Penny Morris**, who loves messing about with engines and keeping fit.

The fire station cook is **Elvis Cridlington**. When he's not fighting fires and trying to cook, Elvis loves playing rock and roll on his electric guitar.

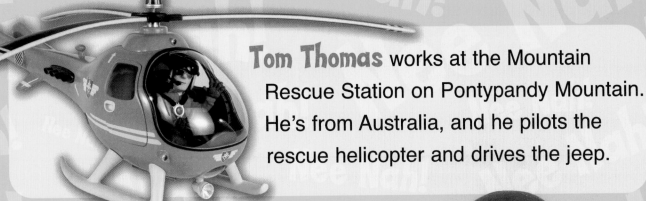

Tom Thomas works at the Mountain Rescue Station on Pontypandy Mountain. He's from Australia, and he pilots the rescue helicopter and drives the jeep.

Mike Flood helps Tom at the Mountain Rescue Station. He's also the Pontypandy odd job man.

Mike's wife **Helen Flood** is a nurse. She travels around Pontypandy in her little white car, and helps with rescues.

Mandy Flood loves having adventures with the crew but she always manages to get herself, and her friends, into trouble.

Pontypandy people

Dilys Price owns the Pontypandy grocery shop. She lives in a flat over the shop with her darling son, Norman.

Norman Price isn't called 'Naughty' for nothing! He just loves being cheeky, telling jokes and playing tricks on people.

Woolly is Norman's pet lamb. He's a bit smelly, but Norman loves him just the same! Read a story about him on page 60.

Trevor Evans is the driver
of the Pontypandy bus. He delivers things all over the village,
and takes the children to and from school.
Can you see Naughty Norman?

Bella Lasagne owns the Pontypandy café.
It's where everyone goes to meet, chat
– and eat her pasta, pizzas and
scrummy cakes!

Bella's cat is called **Rosa**. She's
always poking her little pink nose
into things and has to be rescued
by Sam and the crew!

The Beast of Pontypandy

Dilys Price was in the flat above her shop. She was watching a programme about big black wild cats. "Thank goodness we don't have those beasts in Pontypandy!" she said.

Norman smiled. "Not yet we don't …" he said quietly.

Next day, Norman took Woolly to a field. He stood on one side of a muddy puddle and held out a biscuit. "Here, Woolly!" he said.

"Baaa!"

"Baaa!" said Woolly. He jumped into the puddle and Norman covered him in thick, black mud!

"Perfect!" said Norman. "The Beast of Pontypandy!"

Back at the shop, Norman took a lettuce and rolled it under the bridge. Woolly ran after it. "Look, Mam!" he said. "It's one of those beasts off the telly!"

Dilys saw Woolly's black tail. "Oh, no!" she said.

Then she heard the echo of his bleat: "Baa-aaa-aaaaa!"

"There's a black beast on the loose!" said Dilys. "I'll tell Fireman Sam!"

Sam held a meeting about the beast in Bella's café.

"My Norman saw it first," said Dilys. "Oh, he was so brave."

"Mmm," said Sam. "This beast is probably just someone's idea of a joke. But I still want everyone to take care."

"We're worried about Woolly, Uncle Sam," said Sarah. "We haven't seen him today. You don't think the beast got him, do you?"

"I'm sure he's safe," said Sam. "Let's keep a lookout for him."

"I give-a big-a reward to anyone who help-a catch-a this-a beast," said Bella.

Norman smiled. "A reward," he said quietly. "Great!"

James and Mandy decided to look for the beast on Pontypandy Mountain.

"I'll stay here in town," said Sarah. "We'll use our walkie-talkies to keep in touch."

Norman met James and Mandy on their way to the mountain. He hid Woolly behind a wall.

"Hi, Norman," said Mandy. "We're going to find the beast. Want to come with us?"

"Yeah, cool," said Norman.

Mandy, James and Norman climbed up the steep mountain path. They didn't notice that Woolly was right behind them!

It soon started to get dark. When Mandy heard a sound, she said, "What was that?"

"It's the beast," said Norman. "It's following us!"

"Run!" said Mandy.

They ran along the path, but it came to a dead end. There was a steep drop where the rest of the path should have been! They were stuck!

"Call Sarah on her walkie-talkie, James!" said Mandy. "Tell her to send Fireman Sam!"

Back in Pontypandy, Sarah rushed to tell Dilys what had happened.

"Mandy, James and Norman are trapped on Pontypandy Mountain," she said. "The beast is after them!"

"Oooh!" said Dilys. "The beast has got my Norman! I'll never see his little freckled face again."

"You will," said Sarah. "I'll tell Uncle Sam. He'll save him."

Minutes later, the fire station alarm bell rang. Sam, Elvis and Steele put on their helmets and jumped aboard Jupiter. Her blue light flashed, her siren wailed – **Nee Nah! Nee Nah!** – and they raced off. Penny was right behind them in Venus.

Tom flew the mountain rescue helicopter to Pontypandy Mountain. He lowered the winch and lifted Sam into the air.

"Over here!" yelled Mandy.

Tom lowered Sam down to the path.

"The beast is over there," said James. "In that bush."

Sam looked into the bush and found – Norman and Woolly!

"I … er … saved James and Mandy," said Norman. "Look, I caught the beast."

"**Baaaa!**" said Woolly.

Sam and Penny looked at each other. "Woolly?" said Sam.

Later, Bella gave Norman his reward. It was a huge cake.

"What I don't understand is how Woolly got covered in mud," said Penny.

"And why Norman was all muddy when I saw him this morning," said Sarah.

Dilys looked at Norman. "Have you got something to tell me?" she asked.

"Er … I made Woolly into the beast as a joke!" he said. "Sorry."

Dilys knew how to punish Norman. Can you guess?

"All right," groaned Norman. "Jump into the sink, Woolly, it's time for your bath."

"**Baaaaa!**" said Woolly.

Walkie-talkies

James used his walkie-talkie to call Sarah when he was up on Pontypandy Mountain.

Follow the lines to find out who Sam, Dilys, Mike and Penny are talking to.

Sam

Dilys

Mike

Penny

Elvis

Norman

Trevor

Tom

King of the jungle

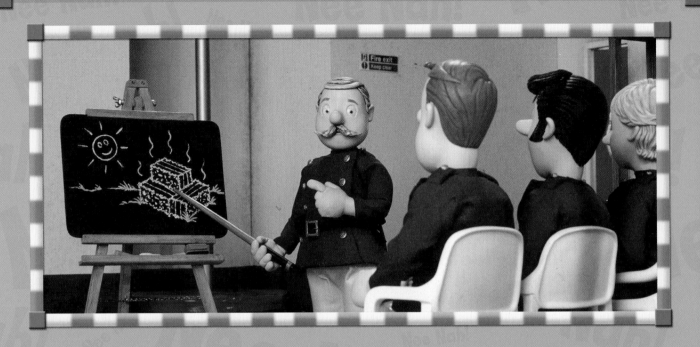

It was summer in Pontypandy. Station Officer Steele was telling the firefighters about how things can burst into flames all by themselves. "It can happen to haystacks in very hot weather," he said. "A warning sign is if the hay smells like toffee."

At the shop, Norman put on his mum's furry bath mat so he looked like Tarzan. **"Aaa-eee-aaa-eee-aaa!"** he yelled.

Sarah and James were pretending to be knights. They had wooden swords and shields.

"Hi, Norman!" said Sarah.

Norman pretended he hadn't heard them.

"You need to wash your ears out," yelled Sarah. **"HI, NORMAN!"**

"Ow, that hurt!" said Norman. "Who you shout at?" he said in a deep voice. "Me not Norman, me Narzan, king of jungle!"

Mandy arrived. "Does your mam know you're wearing her bath mat?" she asked.

"Me no got mam," said Norman. "Me live with gorillas."

He took a banana from outside the shop and ate it. Then he tossed the skin away.

Trevor was delivering a box of tomatoes. He slipped on the banana skin and fell, **ooof!** The tomatoes flew into the air and landed – **splat!** – on James and Sarah.

"Aargh!" said James.

"Yuck!" said Sarah.

"Me sorry," said Norman.

James was cross. "We're going to play knights and you're not invited!" he said.

"Me no want play," said Norman. "Me Narzan, you tomato-heads!"

Norman and Mandy went to the park.

Norman swung on a rope swing. **"Aaa-eee-aaa-eee-aaa-eee-aaa!"** he cried.

"Aaa-eee-aaa-eee-aaa!"

"Can I have a go?" asked Mandy.

"No! You go find nanas for Narzan!" said Norman.

"Get your own nanas!" said Mandy. "I'm not playing!"

"Narzan no need you," said Narzan. "Animals are his friends. Woolly! Dusty! Come!"

"Baa!" said Woolly.

"Woof!" said Dusty.

Norman went off with them. "We go to jungle!"

Out in the fields, the twins found a scarecrow to join their game.

"We are brave knights," said James. "We will attack the castle of evil Baron Blackheart!"

"What castle?" asked Sarah.

James pointed to a stack of hay bales. "That one!"

They fought the scarecrow and threw it to the ground.

Sarah sniffed. "What's that yummy smell?" she said. "It's like …"

"Toffee!" said James, taking a bag from his pocket. "It must be these. Want one?"

The twins didn't see that wisps of smoke were coming from the top of the haystack!

At the fire station, Sam was showing Elvis his new invention. "You stick the broom handle into haystacks. The thermometer on the end tells you how hot they are."

Elvis stuck it into his pasta. "Well, my spaghetti's hot stuff!" he said.

Norman wanted Dusty and Woolly to play jungle animals. But they just wanted to chase their tails!

Suddenly Dusty stopped and sniffed. **"Woof!"**

"You smell trouble?" said Norman. He sniffed. "Me do too!"

He looked around and saw the twins playing near the haystack. It was on fire! "Get away from the haystack!" he yelled.

James saw Norman. "Look, he's waving at us," he said.

"Take no notice!" said Sarah. "I've still got tomato bits in my hair thanks to him!"

Norman had to get help. He raced off to raise the alarm.

"Stop!" he cried when he saw Nurse Flood in her car. "It's the twins! There's a fire!"

"This is a job for Fireman Sam," said Nurse Flood. "I'll call him on my mobile."

"Great fires of London!" said Sam when he got the message. "We've got a hot haystack on our hands!"

Sam, Elvis and Penny put on their helmets and jumped aboard Jupiter. Her blue lights flashed and her siren wailed – **Nee Nah! Nee Nah!** They raced off at full speed.

The twins were still playing when bits of burning hay started to fall on them. "Run!" said Sarah.

James tripped and hurt his ankle, but Jupiter arrived seconds later.

Sam moved the twins to safety while Penny and Elvis hosed down the flames until the fire was out.

Sam pushed the broom handle invention into the haystack. "It's cool now," he said. "It's safe."

Later on, Sarah and James thanked Norman for raising the alarm.

Narzan beat his fists on his chest. **"Aaa-eee-aaa-eee-aaa-eee-aaa!"** he said. **"Me brave Narzan!"**

"Aaa-eee-aaa-eee-aaa!"

Hot stuff!

Can you remember how Elvis tested Sam's new invention? Yes, he pushed it into his plate of spaghetti to see how hot it was!

"Hot stuff!" said Elvis.

These two pictures look the same, but there are 5 things that are different in picture 2. Can you spot them all?

ANSWERS: 1. The letterbox has gone; 2. The stripes on the mug have changed colour; 3. The light switch is missing; 4. A postcard has been pinned to the wall; 5. There is an extra cupboard door knob.

Fit for nothing

You can help read this story. Listen to the words and when you come to a picture, say the name.

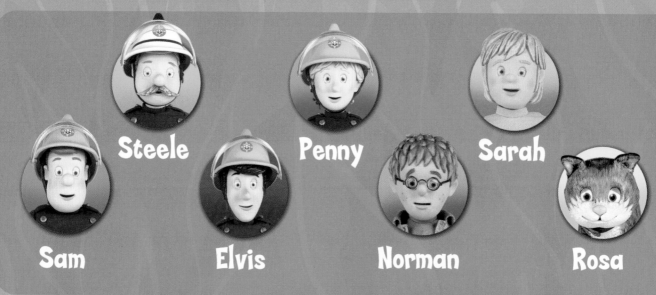

Steele

Penny

Sarah

Sam

Elvis

Norman

Rosa

 shows  his brand new invention. "It's a keep-fit machine," says . "I call it the Joggalator."  and  want to try it.

 tells  that they both want

to be in the Fittest Firefighters calendar.

 sneaks into the gym and

turns the Joggalator speed from

SLOW to **FAST!** Poor

falls off and naughty  laughs!

Then  lifts some weights but

 puts extra ones on the bar!

"Great balls of fire!" says .

There is an emergency!  and  are stuck on the mountain.

"Action stations!" says .

 and  drive off in Jupiter

and follows behind in Venus.

 rescues  but runs

away from ! "After her, !"

says .

They both run after  .

is faster than  , and she catches

 . The next day, a photographer

comes to the fire station. Will he take

a photo of  or  or

for the calendar? No,

the Fittest Firefighter

is  !

Trouble and squeak

One morning, Sam saw Norman carrying something covered in a blue cloth. "What have you got there?" he asked.

"This is the most daringest mouse in Pontypandy!" said Norman. "He can run up a ladder, dive through the air and land in a tub of cheese spread! Meet The Great Squeakendo!"

Mandy sighed. "He's Squeaky, the school mouse," she said. "Our teacher said Norman could look after him for the holidays."

Norman and Mandy took Squeaky to Norman's bedroom. They unrolled lots of rolls of toilet paper and taped the cardboard tubes together. They had made a maze for Squeaky!

Norman put a piece of cheese at one end. "Now, The Great Squeakendo will find his way through the Maze of Mystery!" he said.

But Squeaky's cage was empty. "Oh no!" said Norman. "He's escaped. Where is he?"

Later, Sam showed James and Sarah his latest invention. "It's a grabber," he told them. "The arms get longer so it can grab things that are too high to reach."

"Wow!" said James.

Back at the shop, Dilys was having a cup of tea when Squeaky peeped out of the biscuit tin. He was nibbling one of her biscuits!

"Aaaaargh!" said Dilys.

Upstairs, Norman and Mandy heard a noise outside. They looked out of the window and saw Dilys with a brush. She was sweeping Squeaky out into the street!

"Get out, you little pest!" said Dilys.

Mandy and Norman ran downstairs.

"That's not a pest, Mam," said Norman, as Squeaky ran off down the street. "He's the school pet! I'm looking after him!"

"Oh!" said Dilys.

"Aaaaargh!"

Norman looked everywhere for Squeaky, but he couldn't find him. He made posters with Squeaky's picture on them and took one to the fire station. "His tail's bent and his ears stick out …" Norman told Sam. "I have to find him."

While Norman was at the fire station his teacher rang Dilys. She asked how Squeaky was getting on.

"Oh, he's fine," said Dilys. "Norman's … er … drawn pictures of him. Pinning them up all over town he is …"

Squeaky, meanwhile, went to Bella's café. He grabbed the cheese Bella was about to put on Trevor's pizza!

"Ai-ai-ai!" said Bella. "A giant-a rat! He steal-a my cheese!"

"That's no rat, it's The Great Squeakendo!" said Trevor. "His posters are all over town!"

Trevor tried to catch Squeaky, but he ran away.

Rosa leapt at him and chased him around the café.

"Hissss!" said Rosa.

"Eeeek!" said Squeaky.

"Midoow!"

Just then, Norman and Mandy arrived. "Squeaky!" said Norman. "Grab him!"

But Squeaky was too fast for them. He ran straight up the chimney, and so did Rosa!

"Squeak!" squeaked Squeaky.

"Miaoow!" howled Rosa.

"Oh, no. They're stuck up the chimney!" said Trevor.

"I'll call Fireman Sam," said Mandy.

When Sam arrived he put his new grabber up the chimney and gently grabbed Rosa.

"MIAOW!" said Rosa.

"I've got her!" said Sam.

When Rosa was out of the chimney, Squeaky ran down and Norman grabbed him.

"The Great Escaping Squeakendo!" said Norman. "I'm taking you home!"

When Norman got to the shop Dilys handed the phone to him. It was his teacher again.

"Yes, Miss," said Norman. "Squeaky's fine. We've been playing … er …"

"Squeak!" said Squeaky suddenly.

"That's right, hide and squeak!" smiled Norman.

"Squeak!"

Norman's colouring fun

"Colour in this picture of me and Woolly. Do it carefully 'cos I want to look dead handsome – and so does Woolly! If you do a good job you can write your name on the line."

Norman and
Woolly by

....

46

Draw over the lines, then colour in your picture of Flea-bag – sorry – Dusty!

Dusty by ....

Fiery finale

Sam and Penny were helping Trevor get things ready for the Pontypandy Talent Show.

James was going to make animals from balloons.

Sarah was going to spin a plate on top of a long pole.

Mandy was going to do cartwheels.

But Norman couldn't decide on an act. "What about lion taming with Rosa as my lion?" he said to Trevor. "Or fire eating!"

Trevor shook his head. "I don't think so, Norman."

Tom helped Elvis set up his electric guitar. "Better get the amplifier under cover in case it rains," he said.

"Yeah, water and electricity don't mix," said Elvis.

Station Officer Steele arrived. "Cridlington!" he said. "What are you doing here? We can't all be in the show. Only one firefighter will represent the station … ME! Off you go!"

Norman was still trying to decide on an act. "What about a flea circus, Trevor?" he said. "I've trained Dusty's fleas to do tricks. Look, ready, steady – jump!"

When he heard the word 'flea', Trevor started to scratch! "Norman Price, stop that right now!" he said.

Norman was fed up. He sat down to read his cowboy comic. "Wish I could do tricks like Lasso Kid," he said. "I bet he'd win the show."

It started to rain, and soon there was a big puddle of water on the roof of the stage. But no one noticed …

Norman was watching rehearsals and picked up Elvis' guitar. "How do you turn it on?" he said. He flicked a switch. **Screech!** went the guitar. Norman fiddled with the amplifier. **SCREEEEEEECH!**

"My turn!" he said, running on stage. "I woke up this morning – **TWANG!** – feeling really blue!" **SCREECH! TWANG!** "I didn't know what to do!" Norman sang.

Trevor did! He put his hands over his ears, then grabbed the guitar. "That's enough, Norman!" he said.

"But I want to be in the show!" said Norman. "What can I do?"

"I don't know," said Trevor. "Can't you rope someone in to help you?"

"Hmm …" said Norman. "Maybe I can!"

Station Officer Steele practised his song. "I'm a little teapot, short and stout," he sang. "Here's my handle. Here's my spout."

Norman took no notice. He was untying one of the ropes that kept the roof in place.

As Sarah started to spin a plate, Norman undid the rope and yanked it free.

Whoosh! The water on the roof gushed down on to the stage! Water splashed on to the amplifier and it crackled and exploded, **whoomf!** Then the curtain burst into flames!

"Don't panic!" said Steele. "Trevor, call the station!"

At the fire station, Sam read the message. "We're going to the talent show, after all," he told Elvis and Penny. "The stage is on fire!"

Sam, Elvis and Penny put on their helmets. They jumped aboard Jupiter and her blue lights flashed. Her siren wailed – **Nee Nah! Nee Nah!** – and they raced off to the park at full speed.

"Here's Jupiter now!" said Trevor. "Over here, Sam!"

Sam and Penny ran to the stage carrying the big hose. "Turn her on, Elvis!" called Sam.

Water whooshed out of the hose and soon the fire was out.

"Who switched that amplifier on?" asked Sam. "It's a very dangerous thing to do in this wet weather!"

"Sorry, Sam," said Norman.

When the talent show started, Norman's act was last.

"And now, the boy who made the West wild," said Trevor. "It's Lasso Kid Price and his clever coyote, Dusty!"

"Yee-ha!" said Norman. He spun his lasso into a big loop and Dusty leapt through it!

It was great! The crowd cheered and clapped. "More! More!"

"Well, there can only be one winner," said Trevor.

"Yee-ha!" said Norman. "Yeah, ME!"

"Yee-ha!"

Sam's picture puzzle

Sam and Penny soon put the fire out. Sam told Norman and the others to always remember that:

Water and Electricity Don't Mix

Which of these people can you see in the big picture?
Write a ✔ or a ✗ in each box.

 **Mandy**

 **Woolly**

 **Sarah**

 **Elvis**

 **Tom**

 **Trevor**

 **Bella**

 **Nurse Flood**

 **James**

 **Norman**

 **Steele**

ANSWER: Mandy, Sarah, Elvis, Trevor, James, Norman and Steele.

Mummy's little darling

"Here's a page from my favourite photo album. Funny how all the photos are of Norman, isn't it?"

Who else but my little precious would be hit on the head by a falling sheep?

When Norman dressed up as an alien, he put mushy peas on his face to make it green. Oh, he's so clever!

Why do these things always happen to mummy's little darling? Not fair, is it?

Norman got carried away at Halloween. So did I when I saw Dracula Price! He'll be a big star one day.

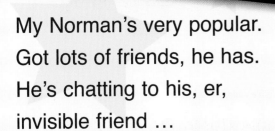

Or maybe he'll join a circus?

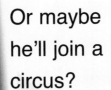

Norman doesn't look too happy, does he? Probably because he doesn't like water!

My Norman's very popular. Got lots of friends, he has. He's chatting to his, er, invisible friend …

Norman always has a wave for his mam. At least, I think he was waving …

The big freeze

It was winter in Pontypandy. Deep snow covered all the streets and roads.

At the fire station, Station Officer Steele said, "This cold weather's a real problem. We can't fight fires with ice cubes!"

Sam poured antifreeze into Jupiter's water-tanks. "This will stop the hoses freezing up, Sir," he said.

At the shop, Norman Price was in his bedroom using Woolly as a pillow.

Dilys came in. "How many times do I have to tell you?" she said. "I don't want that lamb on your bed. Off!"

"Baaaa!" said Woolly, jumping down.

"But Mam, he'll freeze outside," said Norman.

"No he won't," said Dilys. "He's got his sheepskin jacket to keep him warm."

"Don't worry, Woolly," Norman whispered. "I'll find you a warm bed for the night. I know just the place."

The place was Station Officer Steele's office at the fire station!

"This is perfect!" said Norman. "Stay under the desk, Woolly. You'll be warm as toast in here. See you later!"

When Station Officer Steele sat at his desk, he thought Woolly was a sheepskin cushion – until Woolly bleated loudly. **"Baaaa!"**

Steele called Sam into his office. "This is a fire station, not a farm!" he said. "Get that fleecy flea-bag out of here!"

Norman found Woolly out in the cold again. "Don't worry," he said. "Leave it to me. You'll soon be snug as a bug in a rug. Bella's café's warm. Stay there until I've got your bed ready."

Norman ran home. "Mam, I need another blanket," he said. "I was freezing last night!"

"Have this old electric blanket," said Dilys. "I'll plug it in. It'll be lovely and warm by bedtime."

When Dilys had gone, Norman took the electric blanket off his bed and put it on a spare blanket on the floor.

"Mam said Woolly couldn't stay in my bed, but she didn't say anything about him having his **own** bed," he said. "Phew! This blanket stinks a bit – but so does Woolly! He'll love his new bed!"

Norman didn't know that the smell was the electric blanket starting to burn …

When Norman went to the café to get Woolly, Bella was angry. "Your Woolly is-a bully," she said. "Ee push-a my Rosa out-a her bed. Ee 'ave to-a go!"

"But we need something to keep us warm," said Norman. "Can I borrow this tablecloth?"

"Yes-yes," said Bella. "Just-a take-a eem away."

"Norman Price, what are you wearing?" asked Dilys when Norman got home.

"It's a cloak. I'm fr-freezing," said Norman. "I think I'll get into bed to warm up."

"Turn off the electric blanket before you do," said Dilys.

But when Norman opened his bedroom door, the blankets were on fire! He ran back downstairs. **"Fire! Fire!"** he shouted. "My bedroom's on fire!"

"Everybody out!" said Trevor. "I'll call the station!"

"Action Stations!" said Station Officer Steele when he got the message about the fire.

Sam, Elvis and Penny put on their helmets. They jumped aboard Jupiter and her blue lights flashed. Her siren wailed – **Nee Nah! Nee Nah!** – and they raced off to the shop at full speed.

Elvis turned off the electricity. Then Sam took the hose and ran up to Norman's bedroom.

"Water on, Penny!" he called.

Suddenly a long icicle with a sharp point fell from above the shop door. It made a hole in the hose!

"Elvis, the water's off," Sam said into his radio. "What's happened? Over."

"There's a hole in the hose," said Elvis. "Over."

"Use the spare one," said Sam. "Over."

Elvis and Penny fitted the new hose and Sam soon put out the fire.

"Oh, thank you, Sam," said Dilys. "Me and my poor Norman could have lost everything."

"Snugglebun!"

Sam held up Norman's pink rabbit hot water bottle. "Well, at least this little fella's safe!"

"Snugglebun!" said Norman. "You're safe!"

Norman couldn't sleep in his bedroom that night. He snuggled up in the big armchair downstairs.

But Norman didn't get much sleep. Someone kept pulling the blankets off him. Can you guess who it was? Yes, it was Woolly! **"Baaaa!"**

Sam's quiz

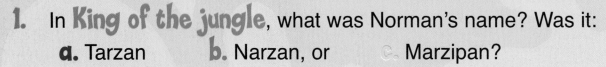

"Try my fun quiz. Look back through the book to find the answers."

1. In **King of the jungle**, what was Norman's name? Was it:
   a. Tarzan   **b.** Narzan, or   **c.** Marzipan?

2. Who did Norman turn into **The Beast of Pontypandy**?

3. Who drives Venus, the rescue tender?

4. In **Trouble and squeak**, what kind of animal was The Great Squeakendo?

5. What is the name of the Pontypandy nurse?

6. In **King of the jungle**, who tested Sam's invention by sticking it into his spaghetti?

7. In **Fiery finale**, who sang, "I'm a little teapot"?

8. What was the name of Sam's keep-fit machine in **Fit for nothing**?

9. Trevor Evans is the pilot of the Mountain Rescue helicopter. True or false?

10. In **The big freeze**, who was Snugglebun?

ANSWERS: 1. b. Narzan; 2. Woolly; 3. Penny Morris; 4. A mouse; 5. Helen Flood; 6. Elvis Cridlington; 7. Station Officer Steele; 8. The Joggalator; 9. False, the pilot is Tom Thomas. Trevor drives the bus; 10. Norman's pink rabbit hot water bottle.

Don't miss Fireman Sam in his own magazine! Packed full of stories, posters and activities.

FREE

Fab free gift with every issue!
The images show typical free gifts

FREE Whistle
Fireman Sam™

Stories • Puzzles • Posters • Fun facts

Use your brightest crayons or pens to colour in this picture.

On sale every 4 weeks

On sale in all good newsagents and supermarkets now!

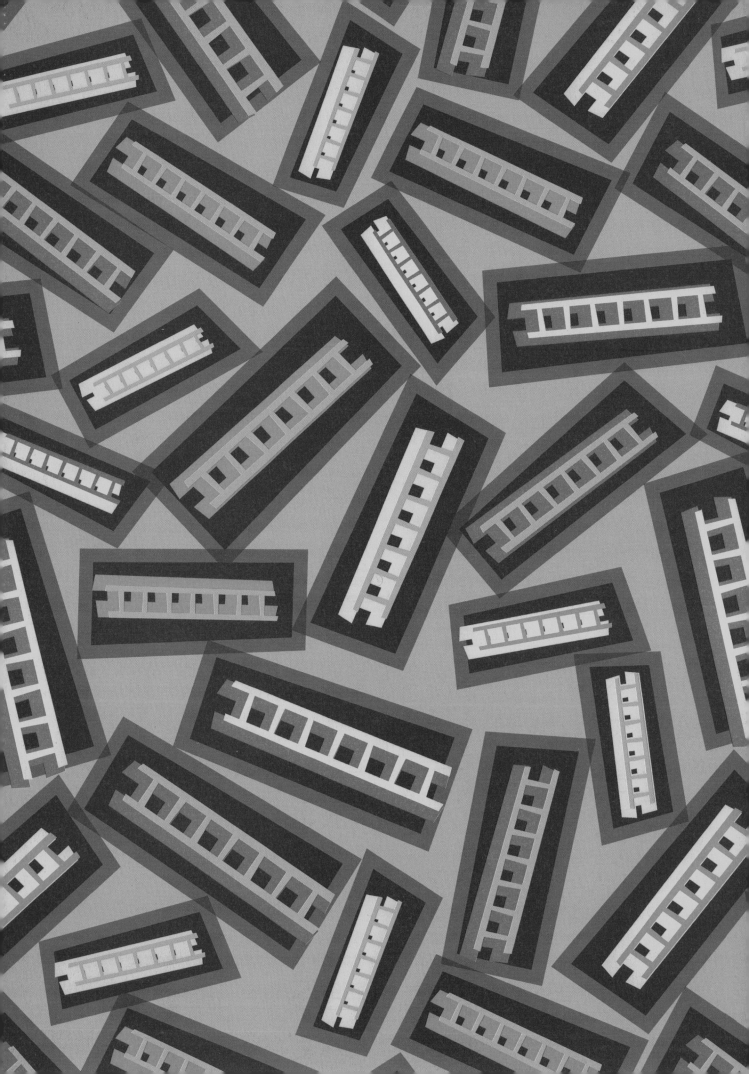